EMMANUEL JOSEPH

From Battlefields to Hospitals, The Role of Cryptocurrency in International Aid Networks

Copyright © 2025 by Emmanuel Joseph

All rights reserved. No part of this publication may be reproduced, stored or transmitted in any form or by any means, electronic, mechanical, photocopying, recording, scanning, or otherwise without written permission from the publisher. It is illegal to copy this book, post it to a website, or distribute it by any other means without permission.

First edition

*This book was professionally typeset on Reedsy.
Find out more at reedsy.com*

Contents

1   Chapter 1: A New Dawn in Aid   1
2   Chapter 2: Empowering Grassroots Organizations   2
3   Chapter 3: Revolutionizing Healthcare Aid   3
4   Chapter 4: Overcoming Political Barriers   4
5   Chapter 5: Enhancing Security in Conflict Zones   5
6   Chapter 6: Addressing Financial Inclusion   6
7   Chapter 7: Streamlining Humanitarian Logistics   7
8   Chapter 8: Promoting Donor Engagement   8
9   Chapter 9: Fostering Collaboration Among Aid Organizations   9
10   Chapter 10: Leveraging Technology for Impact   10
11   Chapter 11: Challenges and Opportunities   11
12   Chapter 12: The Future of International Aid   12
13   Chapter 13: Cryptocurrencies and Disaster Relief   13
14   Chapter 14: Digital Identity and Aid Distribution   14
15   Chapter 15: Reducing Transaction Costs   15
16   Chapter 16: Cryptocurrency as a Hedge Against Hyperinflation   16
17   Chapter 17: Innovative Funding Mechanisms   17
18   Chapter 18: Supporting Economic Recovery   18
19   Chapter 19: Integrating Cryptocurrencies with Traditional...   19
20   Chapter 20: Addressing Technological Barriers   20
21   Chapter 21: Legal and Regulatory Considerations   21
22   Chapter 22: Future Innovations in Aid Delivery   22

1

Chapter 1: A New Dawn in Aid

The advent of cryptocurrency has opened new frontiers in international aid networks. Gone are the days of traditional financial hurdles; today, digital currencies are streamlining the distribution of aid across borders. From Bitcoin to Ethereum, these decentralized systems offer security, transparency, and immediacy that traditional banking often lacks. For humanitarian organizations operating in volatile regions, cryptocurrencies represent a lifeline.

Cryptocurrency enables real-time transactions, bypassing the bureaucracy and red tape that often delays traditional aid. This immediacy can be crucial in crisis situations where every second counts. When funds are needed urgently for medical supplies, food, or shelter, the speed of digital currency transactions can mean the difference between life and death.

Moreover, the transparency of blockchain technology ensures that funds are traceable and accountable. This traceability helps in reducing corruption and ensuring that aid reaches its intended recipients. For international donors and aid organizations, this level of transparency builds trust and fosters a more robust and responsive aid network.

2

Chapter 2: Empowering Grassroots Organizations

Grassroots organizations often face significant barriers in accessing international aid. Traditional financial systems can be slow and exclusionary, often leaving the most vulnerable populations without support. Cryptocurrencies, however, empower these organizations by providing a more inclusive financial system.

With digital currencies, grassroots organizations can receive and distribute funds directly, without the need for intermediaries. This direct access not only speeds up the process but also reduces the costs associated with traditional banking. For many small organizations, these savings can be redirected to more essential services and programs.

Additionally, cryptocurrencies can operate in regions where traditional banks might be absent or dysfunctional. In conflict zones or remote areas, digital currencies provide a reliable alternative to traditional financial systems, ensuring that aid can still flow to those in need. This capability is particularly critical in regions where infrastructure has been destroyed or governments are unstable.

3

Chapter 3: Revolutionizing Healthcare Aid

Healthcare is one of the most critical sectors in need of international aid, and cryptocurrencies are revolutionizing how this aid is delivered. In areas devastated by war or natural disasters, access to healthcare can be a matter of survival. Cryptocurrencies provide a streamlined method for funding medical supplies, paying healthcare workers, and supporting hospitals.

Digital currencies facilitate quick and efficient transactions, ensuring that funds reach healthcare providers promptly. This efficiency is crucial in emergency situations where delays can result in loss of life. Whether it's transferring funds to purchase vaccines or paying for medical equipment, the speed of cryptocurrency transactions can significantly enhance the responsiveness of healthcare aid.

Moreover, the transparency of blockchain technology ensures that every transaction is recorded and can be audited. This feature is essential for maintaining accountability and building trust among donors, recipients, and aid organizations. With clear records, it's easier to ensure that funds are used appropriately and effectively, ultimately improving the overall impact of healthcare aid.

4

Chapter 4: Overcoming Political Barriers

In many parts of the world, political barriers can hinder the delivery of international aid. Governments may impose restrictions, bureaucratic red tape, or even outright corruption. Cryptocurrencies offer a way to bypass these obstacles, providing a more direct and efficient method for delivering aid.

By using digital currencies, international aid organizations can circumvent traditional financial systems that may be controlled or influenced by corrupt officials. This independence allows aid to reach its intended recipients without interference, ensuring that the most vulnerable populations receive the support they need.

Moreover, the decentralized nature of cryptocurrencies means that no single entity controls the flow of funds. This decentralization reduces the risk of funds being misappropriated by corrupt officials or organizations. For international aid networks, this level of security and transparency is invaluable in maintaining the integrity of their operations.

5

Chapter 5: Enhancing Security in Conflict Zones

Delivering aid in conflict zones presents unique challenges, including security risks for aid workers and recipients. Cryptocurrencies can enhance security by reducing the need for physical cash transfers, which can be dangerous and susceptible to theft or extortion.

Digital currencies allow for secure, digital transactions that can be conducted remotely. This capability minimizes the risks associated with transporting cash in conflict zones, where armed groups or criminals may target aid workers. By using cryptocurrencies, aid organizations can ensure that funds reach their destination safely.

Moreover, the use of blockchain technology provides a secure record of transactions, making it more difficult for funds to be diverted or stolen. This increased security helps protect both the aid workers and the recipients, ensuring that aid reaches those who need it most.

6

Chapter 6: Addressing Financial Inclusion

Financial inclusion is a significant challenge in many parts of the world, where large segments of the population remain unbanked or underbanked. Cryptocurrencies offer a solution by providing access to financial services for those who are excluded from traditional banking systems.

With digital wallets, individuals in remote or underserved areas can receive and manage funds without the need for a bank account. This capability is particularly important for marginalized populations, including refugees and displaced persons, who may lack the documentation required for traditional banking.

Cryptocurrencies also offer lower transaction costs compared to traditional banking, making them more accessible to low-income individuals. This financial inclusivity helps ensure that aid reaches the most vulnerable populations, empowering them to manage their finances and rebuild their lives.

7

Chapter 7: Streamlining Humanitarian Logistics

Logistics play a crucial role in the delivery of humanitarian aid, and cryptocurrencies can streamline these operations. From tracking shipments to paying suppliers, digital currencies offer a more efficient and transparent method for managing logistics.

Blockchain technology enables the tracking of goods from the point of origin to the final destination, ensuring that aid supplies are delivered as intended. This traceability helps in reducing fraud and ensuring that resources are used effectively.

Furthermore, cryptocurrencies facilitate quick and secure payments to suppliers and logistics providers. This capability reduces delays and ensures that aid supplies are delivered promptly, enhancing the overall efficiency of humanitarian operations.

Chapter 8: Promoting Donor Engagement

Cryptocurrencies can also enhance donor engagement by providing greater transparency and accountability. Donors want to know that their contributions are making a difference, and digital currencies offer a way to demonstrate this impact.

With blockchain technology, every transaction can be recorded and audited, providing a clear trail of how funds are used. This transparency builds trust and encourages more individuals and organizations to contribute to international aid efforts.

Moreover, cryptocurrencies offer new ways for donors to contribute, including micro-donations and crowd-funding campaigns. These innovative approaches can attract a broader range of donors, increasing the overall pool of resources available for humanitarian aid.

Chapter 9: Fostering Collaboration Among Aid Organizations

Collaboration among aid organizations is essential for maximizing the impact of humanitarian efforts. Cryptocurrencies can foster this collaboration by providing a common platform for financial transactions and data sharing.

Digital currencies enable organizations to pool resources and coordinate their efforts more effectively. This capability is particularly important in large-scale crises, where multiple organizations must work together to provide comprehensive support.

Moreover, the transparency of blockchain technology facilitates trust and cooperation among aid organizations. With a clear record of transactions, organizations can ensure that resources are used efficiently and effectively, enhancing the overall impact of their efforts.

10

Chapter 10: Leveraging Technology for Impact

The integration of cryptocurrencies with other emerging technologies can further enhance the impact of international aid. From artificial intelligence to the Internet of Things, these technologies offer new ways to deliver and manage aid more effectively.

For example, smart contracts enabled by blockchain technology can automate the distribution of aid based on predefined conditions. This automation reduces the risk of human error and ensures that aid is delivered promptly and accurately.

Moreover, the use of digital identities can enhance the efficiency of aid distribution. By providing secure and verifiable identification for recipients, aid organizations can ensure that resources reach the right individuals. This capability is particularly important in regions where traditional identification systems may be lacking or unreliable.

11

Chapter 11: Challenges and Opportunities

While cryptocurrencies offer many benefits for international aid networks, they also present challenges that must be addressed. Issues such as regulatory uncertainty, technological barriers, and cybersecurity risks require careful consideration.

Regulatory uncertainty can hinder the adoption of cryptocurrencies in some regions, as governments grapple with how to classify and regulate digital currencies. Aid organizations must navigate these regulatory landscapes to ensure compliance and avoid potential legal issues.

Technological barriers, including access to digital infrastructure and technical literacy, can also pose challenges. Ensuring that both aid workers and recipients are equipped to use cryptocurrencies is essential for their effective implementation.

Despite these challenges, the opportunities presented by cryptocurrencies for international aid are immense. With continued innovation and collaboration, these digital currencies can transform the way aid is delivered, making it more efficient, transparent, and inclusive.

12

Chapter 12: The Future of International Aid

The future of international aid lies in embracing new technologies and innovative approaches. Cryptocurrencies are at the forefront of this transformation, offering new ways to deliver aid more effectively and efficiently.

As digital currencies continue to evolve, they will play an increasingly important role in international aid networks. By harnessing the power of blockchain technology, aid organizations can ensure that resources are used transparently and accountably, building trust among donors and recipients.

Ultimately, the goal of international aid is to improve the lives of those in need. With cryptocurrencies, we have the potential to do this more effectively than ever before, ensuring that aid reaches those who need it most and making a lasting impact on global humanitarian efforts.

13

Chapter 13: Cryptocurrencies and Disaster Relief

In the wake of natural disasters, speed and efficiency are paramount. Cryptocurrencies can expedite the distribution of relief funds, ensuring that victims receive the help they need without delay. By bypassing traditional banking systems, digital currencies provide a more immediate response to crises, delivering aid where it's needed most.

The blockchain technology behind cryptocurrencies also enables the tracking of funds, ensuring that relief money is used appropriately. This level of transparency helps build trust among donors and recipients, promoting a more efficient and effective disaster response. As climate change increases the frequency and severity of natural disasters, the role of cryptocurrencies in disaster relief will become increasingly important.

Cryptocurrencies also offer the potential for innovative disaster relief solutions. For example, smart contracts can automate the release of funds based on predefined conditions, such as the occurrence of a natural disaster. This automation ensures a swift and reliable response, reducing the time it takes for aid to reach affected populations.

14

Chapter 14: Digital Identity and Aid Distribution

In many parts of the world, lack of identification can be a significant barrier to accessing aid. Cryptocurrencies, combined with digital identity solutions, can help overcome this challenge. By providing secure and verifiable identification, digital identities can ensure that aid reaches the right individuals.

Digital identities can be linked to cryptocurrency wallets, enabling secure and efficient distribution of funds. This capability is particularly important for refugees and displaced persons, who may lack the documentation required for traditional banking. With digital identities, these individuals can receive and manage aid without the need for a bank account.

Moreover, digital identities can help prevent fraud and ensure that resources are used appropriately. By providing a verifiable record of transactions, blockchain technology enhances accountability and transparency, promoting a more effective distribution of aid.

15

Chapter 15: Reducing Transaction Costs

Traditional financial systems often involve high transaction costs, which can reduce the amount of aid that reaches recipients. Cryptocurrencies offer a more cost-effective alternative, with lower transaction fees and faster processing times. This efficiency helps ensure that a larger portion of aid funds is used for their intended purpose.

Lower transaction costs also make it easier for international donors to contribute to aid efforts. By reducing the financial barriers to giving, cryptocurrencies can attract a broader range of donors, increasing the overall pool of resources available for humanitarian aid.

Additionally, the lower costs associated with digital currencies can benefit small and grassroots organizations, which often operate on tight budgets. By minimizing transaction fees, these organizations can allocate more funds to essential services and programs, enhancing their impact on vulnerable populations.

16

Chapter 16: Cryptocurrency as a Hedge Against Hyperinflation

In regions experiencing hyperinflation, traditional currencies can quickly lose their value, making it difficult for aid organizations to provide effective support. Cryptocurrencies offer a stable alternative, providing a more reliable store of value in volatile economic environments.

By using digital currencies, aid organizations can protect the value of their funds, ensuring that they can continue to provide essential services even in the face of economic instability. This capability is particularly important in countries with weak financial systems, where hyperinflation can have devastating effects on vulnerable populations.

Moreover, cryptocurrencies can provide a more stable means of financial exchange for recipients. By using digital wallets, individuals can protect their funds from devaluation, ensuring that they can purchase essential goods and services. This stability helps promote financial resilience and support recovery efforts in regions experiencing economic turmoil.

17

Chapter 17: Innovative Funding Mechanisms

Cryptocurrencies enable new and innovative funding mechanisms for international aid. From initial coin offerings (ICOs) to decentralized finance (DeFi) platforms, these digital currencies offer a range of options for raising and distributing funds.

ICOs provide a way for aid organizations to raise funds by issuing digital tokens, which can be purchased by donors. These tokens can represent various forms of value, such as access to services or voting rights in decision-making processes. By leveraging ICOs, aid organizations can attract a diverse range of donors and raise funds more efficiently.

DeFi platforms offer another innovative funding mechanism, enabling peer-to-peer financial transactions without the need for intermediaries. These platforms can facilitate microloans, crowdfunding campaigns, and other forms of financial support, providing aid organizations with additional tools for raising and distributing funds.

18

Chapter 18: Supporting Economic Recovery

Cryptocurrencies can play a crucial role in supporting economic recovery in regions affected by conflict or disaster. By providing access to financial services, digital currencies can help rebuild local economies and promote sustainable development.

Digital currencies enable secure and efficient transactions, facilitating trade and commerce in areas where traditional banking systems may be absent or dysfunctional. By supporting local businesses and entrepreneurs, cryptocurrencies can help stimulate economic growth and create jobs, promoting long-term recovery.

Moreover, the transparency and accountability provided by blockchain technology can help ensure that recovery funds are used effectively. By tracking the flow of funds and verifying transactions, aid organizations can build trust and promote a more efficient use of resources, enhancing the overall impact of economic recovery efforts.

19

Chapter 19: Integrating Cryptocurrencies with Traditional Aid Systems

While cryptocurrencies offer many benefits, integrating them with traditional aid systems can enhance their effectiveness. By combining the strengths of digital currencies with established financial systems, aid organizations can create a more robust and responsive aid network.

For example, aid organizations can use cryptocurrencies for rapid response and immediate relief efforts, while relying on traditional banking systems for long-term recovery and development projects. This hybrid approach ensures that the unique advantages of digital currencies are leveraged while maintaining the stability and reliability of traditional systems.

Additionally, integrating cryptocurrencies with traditional aid systems can help address regulatory challenges and promote broader adoption. By working with governments and financial institutions, aid organizations can navigate the complexities of regulatory landscapes and ensure compliance, enhancing the overall effectiveness of their operations.

20

Chapter 20: Addressing Technological Barriers

While cryptocurrencies offer significant benefits for international aid, technological barriers can hinder their adoption. Ensuring access to digital infrastructure and technical literacy is essential for the effective implementation of digital currencies in aid networks.

Aid organizations can play a crucial role in addressing these barriers by providing training and support for both aid workers and recipients. By enhancing technical literacy and promoting the use of digital wallets, organizations can ensure that cryptocurrencies are accessible and usable for all.

Moreover, investing in digital infrastructure, such as internet access and mobile technology, can help bridge the digital divide and promote the broader adoption of cryptocurrencies. By addressing these technological barriers, aid organizations can unlock the full potential of digital currencies for humanitarian aid.

21

Chapter 21: Legal and Regulatory Considerations

The use of cryptocurrencies in international aid presents legal and regulatory challenges that must be addressed. Navigating these complexities is essential for ensuring compliance and promoting the broader adoption of digital currencies in aid networks.

Aid organizations must work closely with governments and regulatory bodies to understand and comply with relevant laws and regulations. This collaboration can help ensure that the use of cryptocurrencies is legal and transparent, reducing the risk of legal issues and promoting trust among donors and recipients.

Additionally, advocating for clear and consistent regulations can help create a more supportive environment for the use of digital currencies in aid networks. By engaging with policymakers and promoting the benefits of cryptocurrencies for humanitarian aid, organizations can help shape a regulatory landscape that supports innovation and enhances the effectiveness of aid efforts.

22

Chapter 22: Future Innovations in Aid Delivery

The future of international aid lies in continued innovation and the integration of emerging technologies. Cryptocurrencies are at the forefront of this transformation, offering new and exciting possibilities for delivering aid more effectively and efficiently.

As digital currencies continue to evolve, they will be increasingly integrated with other technologies, such as artificial intelligence, the Internet of Things, and digital identities. These integrations will enable new and innovative solutions for aid delivery, enhancing the overall impact of humanitarian efforts.

For example, the use of AI can help optimize the distribution of aid by analyzing data and identifying the most effective strategies for resource allocation. Similarly, the Internet of Things can enable real-time monitoring of aid supplies, ensuring that resources are used effectively and reaching those in need.

Ultimately, the future of international aid will be shaped by the continued adoption and integration of cryptocurrencies and other emerging technologies. By embracing these innovations, aid organizations can create a more responsive, transparent, and effective aid network, improving the lives of those in need and making a lasting impact on global humanitarian efforts.

CHAPTER 22: FUTURE INNOVATIONS IN AID DELIVERY

From Battlefields to Hospitals: The Role of Cryptocurrency in International Aid Networks explores the transformative potential of cryptocurrencies in the realm of humanitarian aid. This book delves into how digital currencies, like Bitcoin and Ethereum, are revolutionizing the distribution of aid across borders, from conflict zones to disaster-stricken regions. With 22 chapters, the book covers various aspects of this revolution, including the empowerment of grassroots organizations, the enhancement of healthcare aid, and the overcoming of political barriers.

Readers will discover how cryptocurrencies offer a transparent, secure, and efficient alternative to traditional financial systems, ensuring that aid reaches its intended recipients promptly and without corruption. The book also examines the integration of cryptocurrencies with emerging technologies, such as blockchain, AI, and digital identities, to further enhance the effectiveness of international aid efforts. Through detailed analysis and real-world examples, **From Battlefields to Hospitals** provides a comprehensive understanding of how digital currencies are reshaping the future of humanitarian aid.

www.ingramcontent.com/pod-product-compliance
Lightning Source LLC
LaVergne TN
LVHW010445070526
838199LV00066B/6209